Carl Ford Peter
Reynolds, Illi

The Cracked Reader

ACE BOOKS, INC.
23 West 47th Street, New York 36, N.Y.

Copyright 1957, 1958, 1959
by Candar Publishing Corporation

Copyright 1960
by Ace Books, Inc.

All Rights Reserved

An ACE STAR BOOK by arrangement with
the Candar Publishing Corporation, pub-
lishers of *Cracked Magazine*.

Printed in the U.S.A.

From the CRACKED Publisher

Writing a foreword to this book is no laughing matter. I found that out after reading the first draft. After all, what can you say about a book whose very name makes hundreds of thousands of people break up with laughter? All I can say about it is that I wish *Cracked* were such a book! All seriousness aside, since *Cracked's* debut as a slick, satirical magazine back in 1957, it has set a new all-time record. Mainly, the lowest sales in history! But what do we care as long as we bring laughter to millions of people. Well, maybe not millions. And maybe not laughter. But we do *bring* it to people! Now we are bringing it to a whole new audience, thanks to Ace Books. The confidence they have shown us in publishing this collection of the best material from *Cracked* magazine is especially gratifying to us since, at last, we find another outfit with guts.

Now on with the book. If you like it, tell your friends. Better still, go out and buy a copy of the magazine. If you don't like it, keep your mouth shut. In any case, have fun—be CRACKED!

ROBERT C. SPROUL
Publisher of *Cracked*

New York City
April 1, 1960

Nowadays the most publicized figure is unquestionably the one belonging to the French cinematic star, Brigitte Bardot. Pick up any magazine or newspaper and chances are that you'll find at least one picture of her. What with all the passion she inspires, we got to wondering how she might look if some of the great artists of yesterday and today had painted her. So like with a little stretch of our imaginations, we can just visualize...

BRIGITTE BARDOT

as seen by different artists...

AMERICAN GALLIC   *Grant Wood*

THERE ARE NO HANDS   *Salvador Dali*

GIRL WITH TOWEL   *Pablo Picasso*

UNFINISHED PORTRAIT   *Gilbert Stuart*

THE DUCHESS DE BARDOT

Francisco De Goya

9

THE ARTIST'S SISTER — James Whistler

BARDOT — Amedeo Modigliani

Because of its publicity in Cracked, shut-ups have become very popular all over the world—even behind the iron curtain, as witnessed by the English translation of these . . . . .

RUSSIAN

SHUT-UPS

Where else but in Russia can you eat like we do, hah, Natasha?

Shut up and keep scrounging!

The Russian form of government is the best political system in the world. This I believe as a scholar and as a citizen. And furthermore.....

Shut up and talk slower!

We Russians should be proud. We invented everything—the telephone, electric light, wireless, television, cotton gin.....

So shut up and invent a way to escape from here!

Believe It or Nuts

CLARENCE LIBIDO, A JERSEY CITY BOOKKEEPER, **FOUND 10 BRAND-NEW $1000 BILLS IN HIS PIZZA PIE!** TO THIS DAY, THE POLICE REFUSE TO BELIEVE THAT STORY.

PULA KINLAI, A CIRCUS ACROBAT, DOVE OFF A 1000 FOOT TOWER... **INTO A BATHTUB FULL OF WATER!** HE WAS SMASHED TO BITS.

ALVIN HOTCHKISS,

AN ARIZONA SHERIFF, ONCE CALLED BILLY THE KID "A NO-GOOD ORNERY HORSETHIEF"— RIGHT TO HIS FACE!

THE TOWN REMEMBERS IT WELL AS THOSE WERE HIS LAST WORDS..

IF YOU DUG A HOLE 13,796 FEET DEEP ANYWHERE ON THE NORTH POLE— PEOPLE WOULD THINK YOU PRETTY RIDICULOUS!

HIRAM KLOTZ,

OF BROOKLYN, N.Y., JUMPED OFF THE EMPIRE STATE BUILDING! AND LIVED!

HE JUMPED FROM THE FIRST FLOOR.

Since you're a reader of ours, we figure you often had to defend yourself from bodily harm. So like you should know how to fight back we have prepared this little article on the art of self-defense. The material used has been gathered from our own experience, since like we here had to learn how to protect ourselves from being physically attacked — mainly because we put out articles like this one on . . .

JUDO

VULNERABLE SPOTS ON ANATOMY

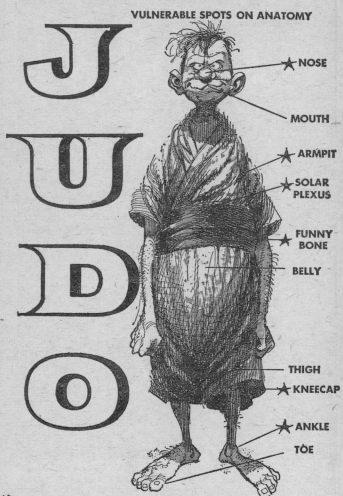

★ NOSE

MOUTH

★ ARMPIT

★ SOLAR PLEXUS

★ FUNNY BONE

BELLY

THIGH

★ KNEECAP

★ ANKLE

TOE

THE NOSE (If he's as big as you)

Jab index finger at point directly under left nostril opening, slicing upward in sudden jerk.

This technique may run into messy complications if opponent happens to have a cold.

THE SOLAR PLEXUS (If he's bigger than you)

Thrust thumb bluntly into midsection, taking careful aim to hit vital pressure point under bottom rib.

Inaccurate aim may cause thumb to stick in belly button, giving opponent chance to club you over head.

17

THE KNEECAP (If he's much bigger than you)

Strike kneecap joint with full five-finger spread, hitting it with swift sharp blow curving slightly upwards.

If blow is not delivered in precise pressure area, knee may jump in reflex action and kick you in gasket.

THE FUNNY BONE (If you're in back of him)

Punch bone at back of elbow with one quick, even shot, making sure jab is made in mid-part of joint.

Since this is funny bone, a sensitive opponent may start laughing, causing stomach to contract — and shorts to fall

THE ARMPIT (If you're in front of him)

Using pointed finger spread, hack away at center of armpit with short rapid stroke directly into crotch.

Should opponent happen to be ticklish, sudden jerk of arm may accidentally punch you in snoot.

THE ANKLE (If you're lying on floor)

Grab ankle bone firmly with clenched fist and twist from side to side in order to down opponent.

Take care that you twist ankle away from yourself, as opponent may topple over and crush you to death.

THERE ARE MANY OTHER LITTLE SIDE GIMMICKS THAT YOU CAN USE IN COMBATING A BIGGER OPPONENT.

THE ARM HOLD

Grab arm at wrist and hack away at elbow. This will empty anything in opponent's hand.

THE LEG HOLD

Grab leg at ankle and flip up over shoulder. This will empty anything in opponent's pockets.

THE BODY HOLD

Grab body at ribs and apply crushing pressure. This will empty anything in opponent's stomach.

Stick fingers in opponent's eye. This causes temporary blindness and he won't see where to attack you.

Pinch opponent on the adam's apple. This causes gurgling and he won't have the wind to attack you.

Tickle opponent under chin. This causes friendly chuckle and he won't even want to attack you.

CORRECT USE OF HAND GRIPS ARE VITALLY IMPORTANT WHEN APPLYING TO SENSITIVE AREAS ON THE BODY

THE ONE-FINGER JAB

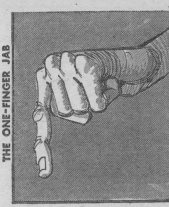

A thrust in the appropriate area will make opponent jump

THE RIB-CRUSHING HOLD

A right fist grip in the appropriate area will make opponent gasp

THE NECK-TWISTING GRIP

A squeeze in appropriate area will make opponent gurgle.

CHART OF DISABLING BLOWS

TYPE OF BLOW	AREAS AFFECTED	REACTIONS
HACK	ADAM'S APPLE	Excruciating Pain, Nausea, Face Turns Purple
JAB	SOLAR PLEXUS	Stoppage of Breathing, Funny Feeling in Pancreas
KIDNEY BLOW	KIDNEYS	Rupture, Hernia, Fidgety all over
RABBIT PUNCH	BACK OF HEAD	Red Face, Loosened Teeth, Followed by Headache
SCRAPE	EAR LOBE	Ticklish Sensation, Then Wax Falls From Ears
PINCH	EYEBALLS	Erotic Sensation, Then Cloudy Vision
SLAP	CHEEK	Opponent Slaps Back
THUMB JAB	END OF SPINE	Opponent Jumps Up
CLAP	HANDS	Opponent Takes Bow

CRACKED takes you back to...

When it all Started

Quick, Archduke Ferdinand, hide in this closet. If my husband ever found you here, he'd kill you for sure . . .

FIRST WORLD WAR

RUSSIAN-JAPANESE WAR

PELEPONNESEAN WAR

25

And now we present our version of a popular television western, which has for its hero a man fast with the gun, sharp with the cards, cool with the chicks, but mainly flashy with the clothes — the man they call ...

BAT MASTEYSON

Bat's here! Git outta the way! Pronto! Bat is comin'! *Vamoose!* Everybody duck! It's BAT! BAT! *BAT!*

Now let's go over to the lunch counter. When Bat Masteyson eats, everybody eats!

Now let's go over and settle our own bills. When Bat Masteyson pays, everybody pays!

C'mon boys, let's go over to the bar. When Bat Masteyson drinks, everybody drinks!

31

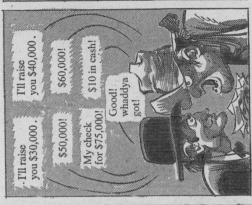

ARE COMICS RUINING OUR CHILDREN?

YES! Says Dr. O. Kropotkin, world famous psychoanalyst. Our comic heroes are all neurotic and psychotic. Children are being unhealthfully conditioned, and tend to develop the fears and anxieties of these characters. In support of his claims, Dr. Kropotkin offers the following analyses of leading comic strip heroes...

DR. OSGOOD KROPOTKIN

LONE RANGER
MASKITIS DEMENTIA

Definite introvert type. Keeps by himself all the time. Won't let others get to know him. Wears mask to conceal probable physical deformity which he feels inferior about. Has formed abnormal relationship with a man called "Tonto," who also shows well-developed psychotic tendencies.

TARZAN
APIS PERVERSIA

Has a strange compulsion to swing from trees. Beats chest wildly and talks to animals. Engages in irregular behavior with a chimpanzee. Unmistakably atavistic nature, due to a severely retarded libido. Finds it difficult to communicate with others, probably stemming from early childhood conflict.

LIL ABNER
DOGPATCHIS HILLBILLIA

Extraordinary case of stunted intellectual growth. Very low I.Q. is seen in his inability to make intelligent rationalization. Probably caused by a faulty upbringing by maladjusted parents. Strong-willed mother who dominates a weak father who eats nothing but pork chops. Clear Oedipus complex.

39

SMILIN' JACK
SILLYITIS GRINNIA

Contrary to name, subject never smiles. Walks around with pained expression on face, indicating excessive melancholia, due to deeply-rooted fears and anxieties. Passion for airplanes suggests immature desire to escape from reality. Unhealthfully attached to "Downwind," a strange narcissistic type.

SUPERMAN
SCHIZOPHRENIA CLARKENTIS

Possesses an extreme split-personality. Overly meek at times, then suddenly becomes a manic-depressive. This indicates a poorly balanced psyche control. Also has a peculiar habit of disrobing in telephone booths. Can be dangerous if let loose.

MUTT AND JEFF
DOUBIS IDIOSIA

A very strange pair. Definitely a neurotic attraction, in which each finds complete fulfillment in the other. Neither ever relates at all to the opposite sex. Standard case of arrested libido growth. A good guess is that Mutt finds in Jeff the father he never had.

ORPHAN ANNIE
LEAPINLIZARDS PRAECOX

Keeps wearing same dress all the time, show ing complete disregard for conventional stand ards. Dilated pupils of the eyes indicate a rare type demented make-up. Claims to hear voices of a dog named "Sandy." Conflict lies in a dis torted Father image, manifesting itself in a "Daddy Warbucks."

MARY WORTH
BUTTINIS NAGIA

Desperately sick old lady who apparently ex periences a neurotic satisfaction in constant ly interfering with the lives of others, mess ing them up considerably. Indicates a sub conscious hostility toward society in general. Maintains a mother-image personality to bring about her sick ends.

POPEYE
SPINACHIS EATIA

Has a neurotic craving for spinach, without which subject cannot function to full poten tial. Going with girl named "Olive Oil" for 16 years and cannot enter into a mature marriage relationship. Instead he finds gratification in company of a paranoic named "Wimpy," who has an odd fetish for hamburgers.

HIP Alphabet Book

Today's children are growing up in a hip world, so like why not start them off early by revising the old-fashioned "square" alphabet book, and coming up with a new-jazzy...

A
IS FOR

Action
LIKE LET'S REALLY ROMP . . .

B
IS FOR

Beat
OF A COOL BLUESY STOMP . . .

H

IS FOR

Hipster

WHO'S A REAL SOLID CAT.

G

IS FOR

Groovy

WHEN YOU DIG LIKE ALL THAT

F

IS FOR

Far out

WHICH IS EVEN MORE KEEN.

I IS FOR

Icky

WHICH MEANS LIKE A SQUARE

J IS FOR

Jivey

LIKE SOUNDS FROM NOWHERE.

K IS FOR

Kicks

THAT'S WHERE YOU HOOK UP

N IS FOR Natch

WHICH IS SHORT FOR "I DIG."

M IS FOR Most

WHEN YOU COME ON REAL BIG

L IS FOR Licks

WHICH GET YOU ALL SHOOK UP.

Q IS FOR

Queen

LIKE THE CAT'S NOT STRAIGHT

P IS FOR

Pad

THAT'S WHERE YOU MAKE IT.

O IS FOR

On

IF YOU'RE "OFF" TRY TO FAKE IT.

T IS FOR **Tough**

WHICH MEANS "COOL" IN BE-BOP.

S IS FOR **Swingin'**

WHEN YOU FLIP YOUR TOP....

R IS FOR **Reet**

IF YOU'RE HIP THEN YOU RATE.

W

IS FOR

Wild

ON TWO YOU'LL BE FIXED-UP

V

IS FOR

Vrootie

AND LIKE ALL OF THAT JAZZ.

U

IS FOR

Unhip

LIKE NOT COOKIN' WITH GAS....

49

Z IS FOR **Zoot**

AND LIKE THIS IS THE END.

Y IS FOR **Yoga**

A NEW KICK WITH A BEND...

X IS FOR **aX**

WHICH LIKE REALLY IS MIXED-UP.

Today the big thing in humor is the "Sick Joke." Many people, however, think that this is a recent phenomenon in American culture. But like "Sick Jokes" are nothing new in our society. The 'Little Willie' verses, written over fifty years ago, were really the very first "sick jokes." And so we thought maybe you'd like to hear what your grandparents used to laugh at, as CRACKED presents . . .

ILLUSTRATED

Little

Willies

Into the well our little Willie
Pushed his baby sister Lily.
Mother couldn't find her daughter:
Now we sterilize our water.

Willie's cute as cute can be!
Beneath his brother, only three,
He lit a stick of dynamite.
Now Bubby's simply out of sight!

Little Willie, mirror gazer,
Found a use for papa's razor;
Sister razzed, "Too young to shave!"
Now they're digging sister's grave.

Willie on the railroad track·
The engine gave a squeal.
The engineer just took a spade
And scraped him off the wheel.

Little Willie, with father's gun,
Punctured grandma, just for fun.
Mother frowned at the merry lad:
It was the last shell father had.

Willie poisoned his father's tea;
Father died in agony.
Mother came, and looked quite vexed:
"Really, Will," she said, "what next?"

Willie in the cauldron fell;
See the grief on mother's brow!
Mother loved her darling well;
Darling's quite hard-boiled by now.

Pity now poor Mary Dillie,
Blinded by her brother Willie.
Red hot nails in her eyes he poked—
I never saw Mary more provoked!

Willie fell down the elevator—
Wasn't found till six days later.
Then the neighbors sniffed, "Gee whizz!
What a spoiled child Willie is!"

Willie saw some dynamite,
Couldn't understand it quite.
Curiosity never pays;
It rained Willie seven days.

Everybody has heard about "Beatnik" parties. They're supposed to be very wild and very intellectual. The conversation is supposed to be stimulating and profound. So like we sent our roving reporter over to a recent "Beat" party and told him to take down a typical conversation, word for word. This is what he overheard, in an article we call . . .

Beatnik

goes

to

a

Party

56

Hey, man!
Haven't seen
you around.
Like what's
been happening?

Everything's cool, Pops!
Real crazy. Still makin'
it with what's her name?

No, Dad! I'm thru with
that chick. She was a
drag. How about you an' ...

Man! She cut
out long ago!
Like I found
out she had
eyes for ...

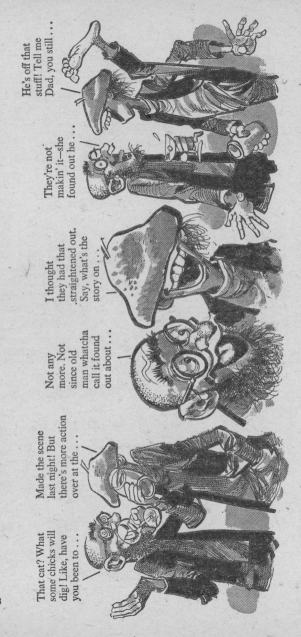

58

59

An Introvert likes to be by himself. An Extrovert likes to mix with other people. To determine just how far out YOU are, take this simple test, and . . .

RATE YOUR PERSONALITY

ARE YOU AN INTROVERT?

Do you seem unable to function well in groups?

Yes [ ]   No [ ]

Do you brood inwardly over every little thing?

Yes [ ]   No [ ]

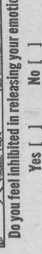

Do you feel inhibited in releasing your emotion
Yes [ ]   No [ ]

Do you hate intrusion of others on your privacy?
Yes [ ]   No [ ]

Do you feel nervous and uneasy moving in crowds?

Yes [ ]   No [ ]

Do you have difficulty relating to strangers?

Yes [ ]   No [ ]

ARE YOU AN INTROVERT?

If you answered 3 of these questions "YES," this means you have a slightly introverted personality. If you answered 5 of these questions "YES," this means you are in a world by yourself. If you answered all of these questions "YES," this means you are really a sad case—'cause you don't take NO for an answer.

SCORE YOURSELF

(Turn over on other side or stand on head to read)

Do you dislike being the center of attraction?

Yes [ ]   No [ ]

66

ARE YOU AN EXTROVERT?

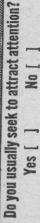

Do you usually seek to attract attention?

Yes [ ]   No [ ]

Do you become restless when you're by yourself?

Yes [ ]   No [ ]

67

Do you always need people around you?
Yes [ ]   No [ ]

Do you tend toward showing off at parties?
Yes [ ]   No [ ]

Do you seem to make friends easily?
Yes [ ]   No [ ]

Do you genuinely like to mix with people?
Yes [ ]   No [ ]

69

ARE YOU AN EXTROVERT?

If you answered 3 of these questions "YES," this means you have a slightly extroverted personality. If you answered 5 of these questions "YES," this means you are pretty far out. If you answered 9 of these questions "YES," this means you are way out—mainly because there are only 8 questions.

SCORE YOURSELF

(Turn over on other side or stand on head to read)

Do you have an open and assertive personality?

Yes [ ]   No [ ]

70

Did you ever have the feeling that you didn't belong? Did you ever have the feeling that you were being looked down upon? Did you ever have the feeling that you wanted to go? . . . . . . What are we saying? Actually, if you don't wear a fraternity pin these days, you're not being looked up to . . . you're a lower class clod. Cracked feels this is unfair, we think everybody should be an upper class clod. So, we came up with our own suggestions for . . .

FRATERNITY KEYS

SUMA COMA AFTER MIDNIGHT

No ethical burglar, sighting this key on sleeping victim, will rob fellow member of his fraternity.

PHI BETA TRASH

Garbage collectors can recognize fellow tradesman in swank cafe, without inhaling surreptitiously.

ALPHA BETA SOUPA

Waiter, alertly observing tell-tale key on diner, will wipe thumb before sticking it into the soup.

PHI BANGUM NOSEUM   BETA URA SHIRT   STIGMA CHI

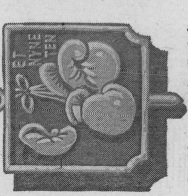

Prizefighter, recognizing disguised champ, can belt him from behind and garner a few cheap, tawdry headlines.

Gambler, who has lost his last cent, can more easily locate someone to refuse him a loan.

Chicken Pluckers, bored, restless, can tar-and-feather each other on alternate Slow Tuesdays.

DELTA SHMELTA GELTA

THE FLUSHEM GUD

Plumber, glomming another plumber posing as millionaire, can expose then bash the phoney in the snoot.

APPLE PI

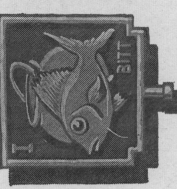

I BITT

One cook, noting another cook incognito, can slip hot food down chap's collar, for want of anything else to do.

PHI BETA SCREAMA

Monster, meeting another monster in dark alley, will team up together and make a movie.

BUMMA SUMA CASH

Beggar, sighting another beggar approaching, can slip key onto his lapel, and save himself from being outrageously pestered.

PHI BETA MAU-MAU

Splendid for little Delinquents so they won't commit faux pas of socking own pals during "rumble."

THETA WAY PARD

Taxi Drivers, meeting one another while both are on foot, can each yell that *they* have right-of-way!

Believe It or NO!!!
BETTER NOT BELIEVE IT!!

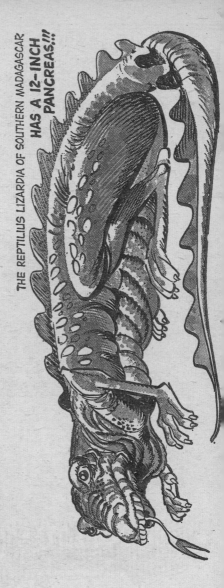

THE REPTILIUS LIZARDIA OF SOUTHERN MADAGASCAR HAS A 12-INCH PANCREAS!!!

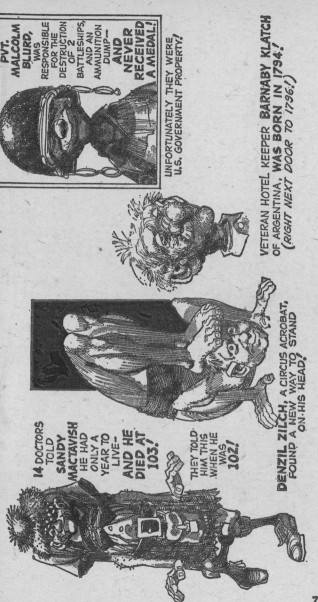

PVT. MALCOLM BLURD, WAS RESPONSIBLE FOR THE DESTRUCTION OF 2 BATTLESHIPS, AND AN AMMUNITION DUMP— **AND NEVER RECEIVED A MEDAL!**

UNFORTUNATELY THEY WERE U.S. GOVERNMENT PROPERTY!

VETERAN HOTEL KEEPER BARNABY KLATCH OF ARGENTINA, **WAS BORN IN 1794!** *(RIGHT NEXT DOOR TO 1796!)*

DENZIL ZILCH, A CIRCUS ACROBAT, FOUND A NEW WAY TO STAND ON HIS HEAD!

14 DOCTORS TOLD **SANDY MACTAVISH** HE HAD ONLY A YEAR TO LIVE— **AND HE DIED AT 103!**

THEY TOLD HIM THIS WHEN HE WAS **102!**

Love is a universal language. It's the same all over the world. Yet in proposing marriage, each nationality has its own individual way—which is indicative of that country as a whole. To show you what we mean, let's take a look at.....

HOW DIFFERENT NATIONALITIES MAKE

MARRIAGE PROPOSALS

I say, Catherine, old girl. We've been seeing each other seventeen years now. About time we had a little chat, what? Frightfully absent-minded of me not to have thought of it before, but perhaps it might be a rather jolly idea to get married. You know, a house, a garden, children and all that rot. Sounds positively bully, what? Take your time, my pet. I shan't need an answer till a fortnight. Meanwhile, what say to a spot of tea? Beastly chilly weather, what? . . .

ENGLISHMAN

Kathleen, me bonnie lass. As ye well know, we hae been courtin' furr nigh on five year now. Prices bein' wha' they are — two con live as cheaply as one. Therefur, I think t'would be a consid'rible savin' furr both of us if we went an' got married. Besides, the tax laws they hae nowadays will make it wort' our while. So wha' I'm askin' of ye, me fair maid'n, is will ye hae me furr ye husband? Now, don't ye be wastin' words. Just answer yea, or no . . . .

SCOTCHMAN

Katina mia, een a leetle while I take my siesta (yawn) but before eet hoppen, I wan' to osk you something (yawn) you know I don' hov mucho dinero (yawn) but I'm pretty good mon an' con take care of woman (yawn) thees is wha' I wan' (yawn) marry weet me (yawn) soon we hov nice l'il house weet mucho bambinos (yawn) an' when everyting quiet down I go get job (yawn) we weel be hoppy (yawn) een 'bout holf an hour wake me up an' (yawn) geev me your onser (zzzzzz) .....

Shh-h! Katrinka, keep it low. There are spies everywhere. If the NKVD ever found out we fell in love, we would end up in Siberia. I know it's just a cheap bourgeois emotion fed to the working class by imperialistic Capitalists, but I can't help the way I feel. I wish I could take you out of the fields and we can get a little collective borscht farm in the country. Let's get secretly married. We can try it on the five-year plan. So help me, Lenin, I love you. Shh-h! Answer by shaking your head...

RUSSIAN

MA CHERIE ... (kiss) ... JE T'ADORE ... (kiss)
(kiss) (kiss) (kiss) ... VOULEZ- ... (kiss)
(kiss) (kiss) (kiss) ... VOUS ... (kiss) (kiss)
(kiss) (kiss) (kiss) (kiss) ... MARRY ... (kiss)
(kiss) (kiss) (kiss) (kiss) (kiss) (kiss) AVEC
(kiss) (kiss) (kiss) (kiss) (kiss) (kiss) (kiss)
(kiss) (kiss) (kiss) (kiss) (kiss) (kiss) (kiss)
(kiss) (kiss) MOI (kiss) (kiss) (kiss) (kiss)
(kiss) (kiss) (kiss) (kiss) (kiss) (kiss) ?
(kiss) (kiss) (kiss) (kiss) (kiss)
(kiss) (kiss) (kiss)

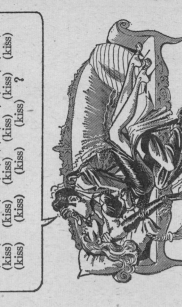

FRENCHMAN

Katy ... sit down ... there's something I want to tell you ... er ... well, it's this way ... um ... there comes a time in every man's life ... no, what I mean is ... you know I don't make much ... I mean ... a fella gets tired of running around ... no, that's not it ... er ... what I'm trying to say is ... I mean, what I want to tell you is ... er ... um ... er um ... gosh ablaze! ... WILL YOU MARRY ME? ... there, I've said it ... so will ya? ... hah? ... will ya ... hah ... hah? ...

AMERICAN

81

LONGFELLOW

We were all sitting around recently, trying to get a little culture for a change by reading some of the world's great poetry. We soon began to marvel at these guys who produced such beautiful works. They must have been inspired very deeply by whatever they wrote about to have created such masterpieces. This started us thinking. Supposin' we had published CRACKED back in those days. Naturally CRACKED would have affected these poets emotionally. They would certainly have written great poems to sing of CRACKED's praises. So like with a little stretch of our imaginations, we can visualize what might happen. . . . .

BROWNING

OMAR

BRYAN

ANONYMOUS
R I P

RILEY

KEATS

MILTON

SHAKS. SHAK.
SHAKESPER.
BACON

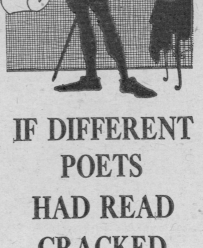

KIPLING

SCOTT

NANOOK

IF DIFFERENT
POETS
HAD READ
CRACKED

CHAUCER

BURNS

HOW DO I LOVE CRACKED?

How do I love CRACKED? Let me count the ways.
I love CRACKED to the depth and breadth and height
My soul can reach, when feeling out of sorts.
To the ends of Being and ideal disgrace
I love CRACKED to the level of Everyday's
Most lowest deed, by dark and not by light.
I love CRACKED freely, as men act when tight;
I love CRACKED purely, as they turn to praise.
I love CRACKED like the poison put to use
In the old days, and with an unbeliever's faith.
I love CRACKED with a love I want to lose, namely—
Like my bad habits—I love CRACKED quite devout
With the malice of all my life! And, mainly—
I would love CRACKED better—if it didn't come out!
E. B. Browning

Breathes there the man with soul so dead,
Who never to himself hath said,
    "This is my CRACKED, my very own!"
Whose heart hath ne'er within him burn'd
As thru the pages he hath turned
    From reading it till it was done?
Is such there breathe, go, mark him well;
For him no minstrel raptures swell;
High though his titles, proud his name,
Boundless his wealth as wish can claim;
Despite those titles, power, and pelf,
The wretch, concentred all in self;
Living, shall forfeit fair renown,
And, doubly dying, shall go down
To the vile Dust, covered and blacked—
With billions of others who never read CRACKED!
Sir W. Scott

A RED RED ROSE

O, my CRACKED is like a red, red rose,
  That's newly crushed in June.
O, my CRACKED is like the melodie
  That's never played in tune.
As far out thou, my bonnie CRACKED,
  So deep in luve am I,
And I will luve thee still, my CRACKED,
  Till a' the seas gang dry.
Till a' the seas gang dry, my CRACKED,
  and the rocks melt wi' the sun!
And I will luve thee still, my CRACKED
  Till the sands o' life cease to run.
So fare thee weel, my only luve,
  And fare thee well bye and bye!
'Cause I don't have to luve thee now—
  The danged sea hath just ganged dry!
R. Burns

When I am dead, my dear ones,
  Sing no sad songs for me;
Plant thou no roses at my head,
  Nor shady cypress tree:
Be the green grass above me
  with showers and dewdrops wet;
And if thou wilt, remember,
  And if thou wilt, forget.
I shall not see the shadows,
  I shall not feel the rain;
I shall not hear the nightingale
  Sing on, as if in pain;
And dreaming through the twilight
  Tho' in the earth I'm lain,
I shall be very happy, 'cause—
  I won't see CRACKED again!
C. Rossetti

ON FIRST LOOKING INTO SPROUL'S CRACKED

Much have I travelled in the realm of books,
And many goodly humor magazines seen;
Round many a newstand have I been
Giving many long glances and looks.
Oft of one publication had I been told
That low-browed Bob Sproul ruled at his demesne
Yet did I never breathe its pure serene
Till I saw the Janitor standing loud and bold;
Then felt I like some watcher of the skies
When a pigeon overhead doth fly;
Or like a house detective when with eagle eyes
He stares thru the keyhole—to see another eye;
You ask how I felt when first looking into CRACKED—
Sick, upon my bed in Darien.
J. Keats

SYLVESTER BEN JANITOR

Sylvester Ben Janitor (may his tribe decrease!)
Awoke one night from a deep dream of geese,
And saw within the gaslight in his room,
Making it rich like crabgrass in bloom,
A clod writing in a book of gold:
An exceptional line had made Sylvester bold,
And to the presence in the room he said,
"Wha-a-a-a?" The clod raised its head,
And, with a look that was racked,
Answered, "I write the names of those who love CRACKED."
"And is mine one?" said Sylvester. "Nay, not so,"
Replied the Clod. Sylvester spoke more low
But drearily still; and said, "If it's not stacked,
Write me in as one that's a lover of CRACKED."
The clod wrote, and vanished. The next night
It came again with a great mazda light,
And showed the names who thought CRACKED was fun—
And, lo! Sylvester's name was the only one!
L. Hunt

Hey, Gang! For those of you who always wanted to draw for a magazine—here's your chance! Run out and get some pen and ink and fill in these blank panels. We cleverly supplied the dialogue. Impress your friends that you draw for us with these.....

DO-IT-YOURSELF CARTOONS

My! That's something, Herman! An elephant carrying a tiger on his back crawling sideways thru the trees followed by a pygmy bushman riding a wooly rhinoceros!

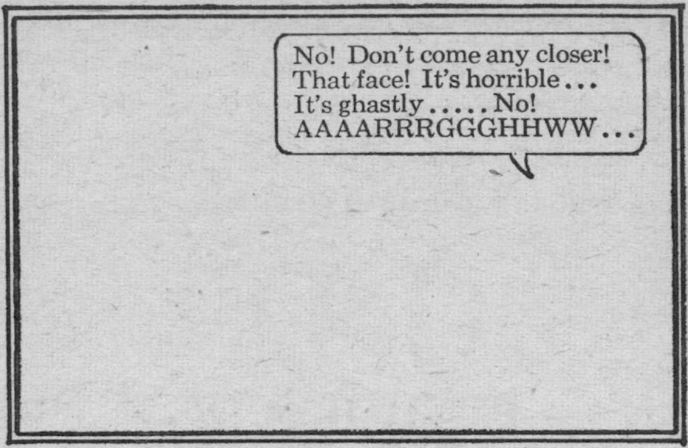

No! Don't come any closer!
That face! It's horrible...
It's ghastly.....No!
AAAARRRGGGHHWW...

Gee! This view of
the Grand Canyon is
breathtaking, Henry!

So you're
the editor
of this
magazine!

It started with the Jack Paar Show. Then Arthur Godfrey switched to the sitting around and gabbing format. This type program has suddenly become very popular.

Suppose everybody got into the act . . . what would happen if all T.V. programs switched to . . .

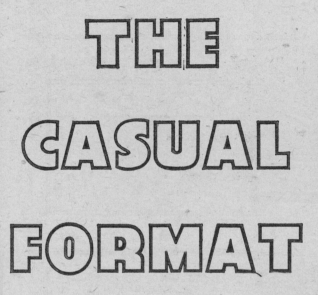

THE CASUAL FORMAT

Good evening, ladies and gentlemen, welcome to another tewst
of the town. We have a reeee-e-
e-lly small one for you tonight.
To open our shew, the world-
famous fire-jugglers, the Arsonis...

Let's all hear it for the Arsonis! Still keeping with our new
relaxed-type entertainment...a
relaxed-type comedian, ladies and
gentlemen...Jack E. Lennard!

Thank you, Ed. I want to say that the last time I saw a face like yours — there was a fish-hook in it! If I was standing I'd tell you more — cause then I could read the cue cards! And furthermore...

Isn't that a wonderful act, folks? Now, still with the relaxed-type format, an act that's really hard to follow... right here on our stage — an explosion of the H-Bomb... Take it away, H-Bomb...

I don't remember eating that!

Folks, if you'd like to see more of these relaxed-type shews, just write in and let us know...

How ya do, ladees an' gennalman. We doin' away weeth our raguler format tonight to jus' sit aroun' an' talk an' let everybody know were not tha bobbling idiots we make out to be on thees show . . .

You're right, Rickey, dear. Let's show our audience that we're not as dizzy as they think we are, and show what we're really like . . .

ON

YOU'RE FOGGING THE LENS!! JIUMBKOFF!

CONTROL ROOM

You absolutely right! An' thot ain't tha way it ees. Les jus' be owselves octing like we *really* are . . .

ON THE

Good evening. I'm inspector Braddock, Bunko Squad. Tonight our program is completely unrehearsed. We're going to talk about one of the most vicious rackets in the country today...

We've exposed many confidence-rackets on this show... right?

Correct!

Uh-huh!

Leeches! Parasites! Unscrupulous men and women who live off human weakness and stupidity, isn't that right?

Sure!

What else?

SHOCK!

Just pick up any newspaper today and what do you see? Violence, bloodshed, and man's inhumanity to man, that's what you see! But like if you pay the newsdealers you won't see these things! All seriousness aside, with the terrible brutalities that go on today, some people are beginning to wonder if the so-called "Primitive" peoples of the world

are really more civilized than we. This started us off on a little investigation of this question. We found out, however, that no matter how much chaos and confusion there is in our society, we're better off than the "Primitives," who are even more savage and barbaric than we are. This is proven in the next article, as CRACKED answers the question ...

ARE WE CIVILIZED?

Civilized people are not bothered by these infantile superstitions in their dress and adornment.

Savages are known to wear bizarre ornaments and outlandish makeup to ward off ary evil spirits.

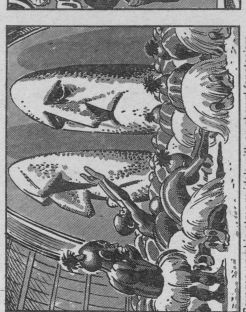

Savages worship strange idols with an absurd fanatacism
that is usually found in infantile or diseased minds.

Civilized members are not slaves to supernatural worship and only believe in those things that are real.

Civilized dancing is based on certain fundamental steps that everyone follows in an organized fashion.

Savage dancing is a violent and a grotesque affair where everyone runs amok in a disorganized fury.

Civilized teenagers go to colleges and universities which are supposed to prepare them for future manhood.

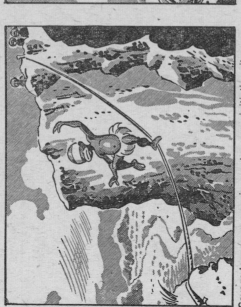

Savage teenagers are given outrageous initiation rites which are supposed to prepare them for manhood.

Civilized men and women always keep active and handle their affairs with a real fixed purpose in mind.

Savages just seem to loll around in the sun all day without any real ambition or fixed purpose in mind.

STORY OF THE YEAR

107

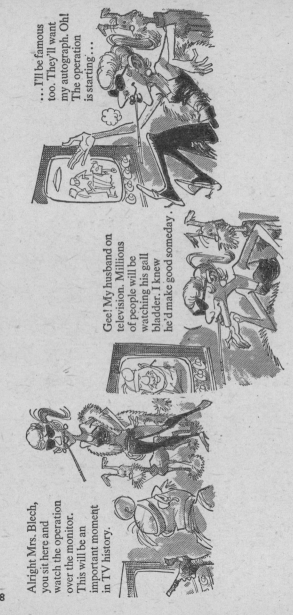

...I'll be famous too. They'll want my autograph. Oh! The operation is starting....

Gee! My husband on television. Millions of people will be watching his gall bladder. I knew he'd make good someday.

Alright Mrs. Blech, you sit here and watch the operation over the monitor. This will be an important moment in TV history.

109

Frozen Rip Van Winkles?

Los Angeles, Feb. 17 (AP)—Experiments to determine if man can be frozen solid for years—long trips to other solar systems are under way at the University of California at Los Angeles.

Dr. John Lyman of UCLA's bio-technology laboratory plans to freeze mice and rats first, but believes his findings can be used to turn humans into ice-like statues for ageless trips through space.

"The big problem is not getting man into space," Dr. Lyman said yesterday. "That will be done within a very few years. The problem is to keep him from becoming psychotic—going insane—under the unnatural conditions and confinement of space flight."

Giving man a natural environment—building space ships big enough to provide oxygen, food and social and recreational facilities—may be prohibitive in cost.

The best answer, he said, is frozen sleep. The voyager would not need food, oxygen or companionship. His ship would be operated by electronic brains and he would be revived by an automatic warming process as he neared his destination.

Within two weeks, Dr. Lyman and his associates will begin dunking mice in dry ice-and-alcohol baths to reduce their temperatures to as low as 100 degrees below zero.

"Experiments with monkeys have shown that their temperature can be lowered to 39.2 degrees for up to two hours without detectable after-effects," Dr. Lyman said. "The monkeys, however, were merely in a stage of hibernation.

"What we want to do is stop the life processes completely, then resume them at will.

"If we can do this with man, he will arrive at a distant star—which might take him several normal lifetimes to reach—not one day older than he was when he left earth."

Another frozen sleep would bring the space traveler home years or even centuries after his departure, said Dr. Lyman, and he would have aged only for the period between frozen sleeps.

The idea of freezing living beings solid is not new. But no human nor animal has ever been frozen to the point that Dr. Lyman contemplates. Why does Dr. Lyman think he can suceed?

"Previous experiments with low temperature indicate that certain bio-chemical processes continue even after the heartbeat has stopped," he said. "We believe these minute functions in the cells must be stopped at the same time if the animal is to be revived successfully. Reprinted from THE NEW YORK POST

We happened to pick up a copy of the Sunday Times recently (which is quite a feat in itself) mainly to look thru the want ads for jobs to supplement our income from CRACKED (which is quite a defeat in itself) when we came upon a little article on page 796 (which is quite remarkable since there were only 483 pages). This item told of experiments already concluded whereby they inject a fluid into pilots which freezes them just before taking off in jet planes, so they can stand the atmospheric pressures of high altitude flying. When they reach a certain height, the pilots automatically thaw out and return to normal. All this is in preparation for flights to the moon. This started us thinking (which is about the most remarkable thing yet) since this freezing process is not science fiction but actually in successful operation, why should it only be restricted to interplanetary space travel? Why not commercialize this freezing principle and use it in everyday life? Why not have self-administered freezing tools, like those shown at the right? Why not a CRACKED article on....

FREEZING PEOPLE

FREEZING PEOPLE CAN BE PUT TO VERY PRACTICAL USE IN OUR EVERYDAY LIVES

The cop on the beat is never around when you need him. A frozen cop on each corner can quickly be thawed out in times of emergency.

Classrooms are overly crowded. By freezing half of the students until adequate teaching facilities are available, everyone has a chance to learn.

Babies always arrive at the wrong time—like when father just lost his job, or mother is out-of-town. Freezing baby until times are good would help.

THE FREEZING PROCESS COULD BE HELPFUL FOR SPECIFIC PROBLEMS OF SPECIFIC PEOPLE

People who always get hot under the collar, can freeze their necks before leaving the house.

Wolves can keep their girls locked in a freezer, and thaw one of them out whenever he wants her.

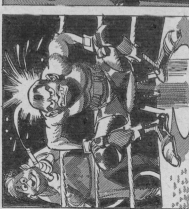

Fighters can be frozen until they step into the ring, to avoid getting out of their peak condition.

THE FREEZING IDEA CAN ALSO BE USED IN DEALING WITH SOCIAL OUTCASTS

Criminals can be frozen and placed into cells until their time is up to save taxpayers' money.

Psychotics can be frozen and quieted down until they are ready to be given proper medical aid.

Magazine editors can be frozen and set aside until they come up with a little better articles.

THE FREEZING OF PEOPLE CAN PROVE VERY BENEFICIAL DURING IRREGULAR WEATHER

During very hot weather people can freeze bodily parts to keep themselves cool, as frost repels sun.

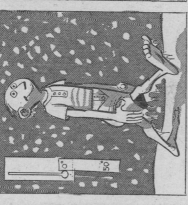

During very cold weather same process will enable people to keep themselves warm, as body heat is reduced.

During very rainy weather people may run into a little difficulty, as whole "megillah" crumbles.

Movie actresses can use freezing so that they don't fade, and thus they preserve their talents.

Housewives can freeze their hips so that they don't bulge, and thus they preserve their shapes.

Career women can freeze their faces so that they don't wrinkle, and thus they preserve their beauty.

THE FREEZING FAD IS BOUND TO BECOME A PART OF AMERICAN FAMILY LIFE

Worried parents can freeze their ugly daughters until they can find them husbands, before they get too old.

Jealous husbands can freeze their attractive wives until they return home from office, to make sure they're faithful.

Clever teenagers can freeze their unsuspecting parents until they get home way past bedtime, after a night on the town.

DIFFERENT PARTS OF THE BODY CAN BE FROZEN TO HELP DIFFERENT PEOPLE

Hand of hitchhiker can be frozen to prevent it from getting tired, while he is out thumbing for a ride.

Hair of guy starting to get bald can be frozen and kept as is, so that it won't be able to fall off.

Since cold contracts, freezing is also of great value to fat women, who like to walk around in slacks.

FREEZING CAN PROVE MOST HELPFUL IN CURING AGGRAVATING INFLICTIONS

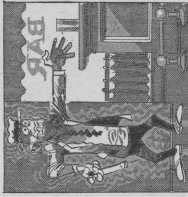

Insomnia can be cured by freezing yourself to sleep instead of by drugs.

Reducing can be brought about in contracting the stomach by freezing it.

The nervous shaking of hands can also be relieved by the use of this process.

BAD HABITS CAN QUICKLY BE BROKEN BY THE USE OF FREEZING TECHNIQUES

The habit of nail-biting can easily be broken by freezing the lips.

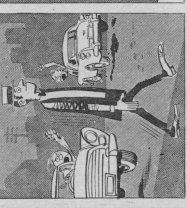

The habit of slouching can easily be broken by freezing the spine.

Trouble is, you easily acquire new habit of over-freezing yourself.

TREATMENT CAN ALSO BE ADMINISTERED TO ANIMALS WHO PRESENT PROBLEMS

Parakeets can be frozen for the night so that you can get some sleep.

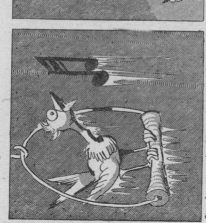

Skunks can be frozen in certain vital sections for certain vital reasons.

Rabbits can be frozen periodically—mainly so there won't be so danged many around.

IN TIME OF WAR THE FREEZING PRINCIPLE COULD HAVE MANY ADVANTAGES

Freeze-weapons could replace bullets and bayonets, and incapacitate the enemy instead of killing him off.

Frozen prisoners-of-war would then be kept in large freezer-camps, so that cost of upkeep is saved.

This may itself lead to war however, as it completely disrupts all the international economic systems.

IF LEFT UNCHECKED HOWEVER, SEVERE DAMAGE COULD BE DONE TO THE WORLD

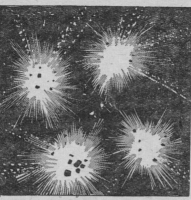

This gap would cause a change in orbit gravitational pulls, resulting in all planets colliding, and destroying the entire universe.

Tremendous frost would cause the earth to contract and grow smaller and smaller until finally it would disappear altogether.

Too much freezing would soon turn huge areas into solid blocks of ice that could spread out and cover the whole earth.

SO LIKE DON'T BE A CLOD AND TAKE CHANCES! PROTEST IMMEDIATELY AGAINST THESE FREEZING EXPERIMENTS! THE WORLD CAN BE DESTROYED BECAUSE OF ALL THIS JAZZ!

A recent poll conducted among neurotics, in various states of hallucination, showed that more of these disturbed people laughed at the following, than any other . . .

CARTOONS

OF THE YEAR

"Dont anybody move — this is a stick-up!"

"EHHH....why should I bother you with my personal problems?"

"Do you expect me to believe a story like that?"

"I'm warning you! No missionary — no dessert!"

"That's my son — the doctor!"

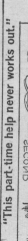

"This part-time help never works out."

"Have you any identification, sir?"

When it all Started

Now, Charles, take the nice gun mommy bought you and go out and play cops and robbers!

Do you think it's a good idea, exposing your son to violence at such an early age, Mrs. Luciano?

People watching television today are being handed a lot of malarkey. What they're getting is a false picture of the Old West. On television all the cowboy heroes are big and strong and clean, but like in real life they were completely different. After a lot of research on the subject, we came across these . . . .

TV
AND
REAL-LIFE
WESTERN
HEROES

SEVERIN

THE REAL-LIFE
BILLY THE KID

TV'S
BILLY THE KID

THE REAL-LIFE
WILD BILL HICKOCK

TV'S
WILD BILL HICKOCK

TV'S
BOUNTY
HUNTER

THE REAL-LIFE
BOUNTY HUNTER

We've given you Space Shut-Ups,
Bop Shut-Ups, Russian Shut-Ups,
now we give you...

CELEBRITY

SHUT
-UPS

Time now for the CRACKED version of a television show that many people feel is all washed up. A television program that you can get water on the brain watching. This is because the actors all haunt the bottom of the sea. So like naturally it's called . . .

SEA HAUNT

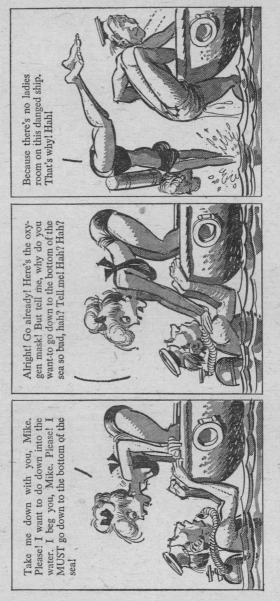

You sent for me, gentlemen? What exciting adventure have you got in store for me? Which deep mystery have you got for me to solve? Mainly, how much money have you got in the bank to make it worth my while?

Darn these women! They always want to go powder their noses. With me it's strictly business! Lemme see if I can make me some loot on this big salvage deal.

Last week I accidentally dropped a suitcase overboard right about here in these waters. I want you to go down and bring it up. It isn't very valuable but it has a great sentimental value for me. It's a large brown valise. I'm prepared to pay you $1000 if you find it....

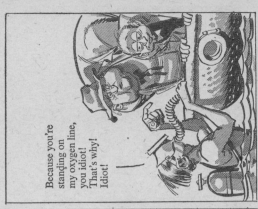

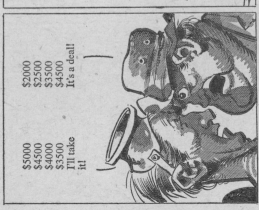

146

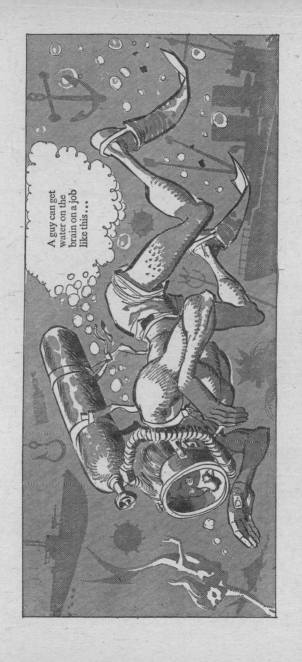

Here's another suitcase. Looks like it fell out of an airplane. Got the baggage sticker still on it. I'll open it up anyway. Maybe it's the one...

Darn that Buster Crabbe and his practical jokes! I'm gonna smash this thing to bits!

150

First let me open it and see for myself. At last! I've found it!

Here (puff) is the suitcase you (pant) wanted. There's a fortune inside. I already (puff) opened it. So where's (pant) the $1000 you (puff) promised me?

I'm glad I'm coming up for air already because my oxygen is low. Also because my body is getting cold. Mainly because the artist is running out of underwater gimmicks to draw.

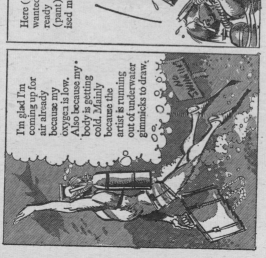

Band-Aids used to be big and bulky. Today they're small and inconspicuous because they're flesh-colored and don't show. Yet this still hasn't solved the problem. There are a lot of people around who have the kind of skin that make these band-aids still stand out. So like we offer a few suggestions on . . .

BAND-AIDES FOR WIERD COLOR SKIN

FOR FRECKLED SKIN

FOR SUNBURNED SKIN

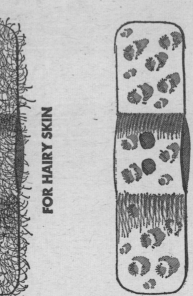

FOR HAIRY SKIN

FOR POCK-MARKED SKIN

FOR TATTOOED SKIN

FOR DIRTY SKIN

FOR HIVEY SKIN

FOR VARICOSE-VEINED SKIN

A couple of issues back we showed you how the most publicized figure of the day, Brigitte Bardot, might have looked to different artists. Now, in answer to many requests (from the artist who wanted to do this bit again) Cracked shows you how the least publicized figure of the day, our janitor, might have inspired great works of art, as we visualize....

SYLVESTER P. SMYTHE

AS SEEN BY DIFFERENT ARTISTS

THE JANITOR IN HIS CELLAR *Vermeer*

THE WHITE BOY *Gainsborough*

POORTRAIT   *Stuart*

PORTRAIT OF A JANITOR   *Rembrandt*

THE DISHES THROWER

Rodin

THE THINKER

THE EIGHTH DWARF   *Disney*

THE GREAT STINX   *Cheops*